Frederick William True

Suggestions to the Keepers of the U.S.

Life-saving stations, light-houses, and light-ships; and to other observers,

relative to the best means of collecting and preserving specimens of

whales and porpoises

Frederick William True

Suggestions to the Keepers of the U.S.
Life-saving stations, light-houses, and light-ships; and to other observers, relative to the best means of collecting and preserving specimens of whales and porpoises

ISBN/EAN: 9783337328917

Printed in Europe, USA, Canada, Australia, Japan

Cover: Foto ©Suzi / pixelio.de

More available books at **www.hansebooks.com**

[EXTRACTED FROM THE ANNUAL REPORT OF THE COMMISSIONER OF FISH AND FISHERIES FOR 1883.]

SUGGESTIONS

TO THE

KEEPERS

OF THE

U. S. LIFE-SAVING STATIONS, LIGHT-HOUSES, AND LIGHT-SHIPS;

AND TO

OTHER OBSERVERS,

RELATIVE TO THE BEST MEANS OF

COLLECTING AND PRESERVING SPECIMENS

OF

WHALES AND PORPOISES.

BY FREDERICK W. TRUE,

CURATOR OF MAMMALS IN THE U. S. NATIONAL MUSEUM.

WASHINGTON:
GOVERNMENT PRINTING OFFICE.
1884.

00.—SUGGESTIONS TO THE KEEPERS OF THE U. S. LIFE-SAVING STATIONS, LIGHT-HOUSES, AND LIGHT-SHIPS, AND TO OTHER OBSERVERS, RELATIVE TO THE BEST MEANS OF COLLECTING AND PRESERVING SPECIMENS OF WHALES AND PORPOISES.

By Frederick W. True,

Curator of Mammals in the U. S. National Museum.

ANALYSIS.

[1]

PREFACE.

On account of the orders recently issued to the keepers of the life-saving stations by Superintendent S. I. Kimball, and to the keepers of the light-stations by Vice-Admiral Stephen C. Rowan, U. S. N., requesting that the stranding of large animals on the coast should be immediately telegraphed to the Smithsonian Institution, it has been thought desirable to offer certain suggestions as to the best mode of telegraphing, preserving specimens, &c., for the guidance of observers.*

---

*CIRCULAR.—ASSISTANCE TO COMMISSION OF FISH AND FISHERIES.

[1883. Department No. 10. Life-Saving Service.]

TREASURY DEPARTMENT, U. S. LIFE-SAVING SERVICE,
Washington, D. C., February 2, 1883.

To the Keepers and Crews of U. S. Life-Saving Stations :

Your attention is called to the following letter, addressed to this office by Prof. Spencer F. Baird, U. S. Commissioner of Fish and Fisheries, and you are requested to render him all the assistance possible in furtherance of the objects specified therein not incompatible with the performance of your regular duties.

S. I. KIMBALL,
General Superintendent.

U. S. COMMISSION OF FISH AND FISHERIES,
Washington, D. C., November 13, 1882.

DEAR SIR : I beg leave to call your attention to a service, in the interest of science and of the fishing industry, that can readily be rendered by those connected with the life-saving stations.

As United States Commissioner of Fish and Fisheries, I am desirous of obtaining a complete collection (to be deposited in the National Museum) of illustrations of the various marine animals the occurrence or capture of which is only occasional. I refer more particularly to whales, porpoises, blackfish, grampuses, and the various other forms of the whale family. These are frequently thrown ashore by the storms, or stranded in shoals, or taken in weirs, but, beyond exciting a passing interest on the part of the bystanders, very little further is heard of them. In addition to these I may mention the great basking or bone shark, and any unknown or unidentified marine monsters, such as might possibly suggest the idea of the far-famed "sea-serpent."

I would ask, therefore, that instructions be given to the persons connected with the Life-Saving Service, during the period of official duty or at other times, to advise me promptly, by telegraph, of the appearance, in their vicinity, of any such animals, and to endeavor to keep them in proper condition, and prevent their being cut or otherwise mutilated until I can send some word. I would cheerfully pay the full value of the oil or blubber of these animals, so that there might be no inducement to cut them up. A telegram sent to the nearest station, addressed "Professor Baird, Washington, D. C.," will come to me without prepayment being required if marked "Government business, collect." If out of the reach of the telegraph, the announcement may be-

The instructions herewith published relate to the cetaceans only, since it is to this group that a large proportion of the specimens hereafter obtained will in all probability belong, and also because requests for information concerning these animals have been already received from several keepers of stations. Similar requests having been also made by a number of captains of whaling-vessels, and by other persons, it has seemed best to make the suggestions available for all classes of observers.

The knowledge of the cetaceans has always been deficient, owing to the difficulty of obtaining a sufficient number of specimens and the

---

sent by mail. On receipt of this communication, which should give some idea of the nature and condition of the specimen, I will at once respond—in some cases sending an expert to prepare the specimen for the Museum.

Some of these animals, if not too large, can be forwarded directly to Washington; others I may wish to have cast in plaster on the spot and the skeleton only removed.

I would also be glad to be informed, in a similar manner, of the first appearance, at tolerably long intervals, of schools of mackerel, menhaden, bluefish, porpoises, blackfish, &c.

Very truly yours,

SPENCER F. BAIRD.

S. I. KIMBALL, Esq.,
    Gen'l Sup't Life-Saving Service, Washington.

CIRCULAR.—ASSISTANCE TO COMMISSION OF FISH AND FISHERIES.

[1883. Department No. 12. L.-H. Board No. 2, of 1883.]

TREASURY DEPARTMENT,
OFFICE OF THE LIGHT-HOUSE BOARD,
Washington, D. C., February 13, 1883.

To the Keepers of Light-stations:

Your attention is called to the following letter addressed to this office by Prof. Spencer F. Baird, U. S. Commissioner of Fish and Fisheries, and you are requested to render him all the assistance possible in furtherance of the objects specified therein not incompatible with the performance of your regular duties.

STEPHEN C. ROWAN,
    Vice-Admiral, U. S. N., Chairman.

U. S. COMMISSION OF FISH AND FISHERIES,
Washington, D. C., November 13, 1882.

DEAR SIR: I beg leave to call your attention to a service, in the interest of science and of the fishing industry, that can readily be rendered by those connected with the Light-House Service.

As United States Commissioner of Fish and Fisheries, I am desirous of obtaining a complete collection (to be deposited in the National Museum) of illustrations of the various marine animals the occurrence or capture of which is only occasional. I refer more particularly to whales, porpoises, blackfish, grampuses, and the various other forms of the whale family. These are frequently thrown ashore by the storms, or stranded in shoals, or taken in weirs, but, beyond exciting a passing interest on the part of the bystanders, very little further is heard of them. In addition to these, I may mention the great basking or bone shark, and any unknown or unidentified lack of room in which to store or display them. It is believed that the zeal displayed by a few American collectors if extended to others will greatly aid in removing the obscurity in which the cetaceans are involved, while in the National Museum may be found a suitable and ample storehouse for the material gathered.

The subjoined instructions have been drawn up by Mr. Frederick W. True, curator of mammals in the National Museum.

S. F. BAIRD,

Secretary of the Smithsonian Institution
and U. S. Fish Commissioner.

---

marine monsters, such as might possibly suggest the idea of the far-famed "sea-serpent."

I would ask, therefore, that instructions be given to the persons connected with the Light-House Service to advise me promptly, by telegraph, of the appearance, in their vicinity, of any such animals, and to endeavor to keep them in proper condition, and prevent their being cut or otherwise mutilated until I can send some word. I would cheerfully pay the full value of the oil or blubber of these animals, so that there might be no inducement to cut them up. A telegram sent to the nearest station, addressed "Professor Baird, Washington, D. C.," will come to me without prepayment being required if marked "Government business, collect." If out of the reach of the telegraph, the announcement may be sent by mail. On receipt of this communication, which should give some idea of the nature and condition of the specimen, I will at once respond—in some cases sending an expert to prepare the specimen for the Museum.

Some of these animals, if not too large, can be forwarded directly to Washington; others I may wish to have cast in plaster on the spot and the skeleton only removed.

I would also be glad to be informed, in a similar manner, of the first appearance, at tolerably long intervals, of schools of mackerel, menhaden, bluefish, porpoises, blackfish, &c.

Very truly, yours,

SPENCER F. BAIRD.

Vice-Admiral STEPHEN C. ROWAN, U. S. N.,
Chairman of the Light-House Board, Washington, D. C.

INTRODUCTION.

The following instructions are intended primarily for the use of the keepers of the life-saving and light stations on the coast of the United States, but an attempt has been made to render them also available for all other persons who may be interested in collecting cetaceans. It is hoped that they are sufficiently clear, brief, and free from technical terms to render them intelligible to any person who carefully reads them. In the course of the development of their craft whale-fishermen have found it necessary and convenient to use a certain number of words in a special sense to designate different parts of a whale, but only a very few of these are used in this paper, and then with the proper explanation.

One great source of difficulty which zoölogists encounter in the study of whales and porpoises lies in the fact that in a large number of instances the external form of a species is known while the skeleton is not; or that the skull or skeleton has been collected but no notice taken of the external appearance. Observers would do well to hold this constantly in mind and to remember that if they are only able to collect, for example, the skull of a porpoise they will add immensely to its value by stating whether the animal to which it belonged had a rounded or pointed head, a hump or a fin on the back, or any other of the important external characters which are briefly summed up on p. 10.

Measurements and drawings also prove of the highest interest, since they frequently help to bring out certain important points which even a long description might fail to make clear.

A more careful study of the various kinds of whales and porpoises is sure to lead not only to a better knowledge of their natural relationships, out to a clearer understanding of their commercial value. There are indications of the presence on our coasts of a number of species, especially of the smaller kinds of cetaceans, which, if better known, might be made the basis of profitable industries.

In a recently published catalogue* I estimated the number of known kinds or species of whales and porpoises frequenting the coasts of North America at sixty-two, but in reviewing the matter again I am convinced that not more than fifty-six can with propriety be included in the list. Even of these fifty-six nominal species fully one-third rest upon no certain basis, and the question of their identity is an open one.

---

* Special Catalogue of the London Fisheries Exhibition, section H, p. 7, Washington, 1884.

[7]

Only about eighteen species can be considered to be well-known, and the majority of these are forms which occur in European waters as well as on our own coasts, and have long been under observation. The number of species whose habits, variations, and distribution are thoroughly understood is still smaller. The commonest porpoise on our eastern coast is the so-called "herring-hog," "puffing pig," or "harbor porpoise," known to science as *Phocœna communis* (fig. 12, pl. iv). Another species which is also very common is the "bottle-nose dolphin," *Tursiops tursio* (fig. 6, pl. ii). The common dolphin, *Delphinus delphis* (fig. 7, pl. iii), which has been known from time immemorial, the black-fish, *Globiocephalus melas* (fig. 18, pl. vi), and a striped porpoise also appear to be very abundant along the Atlantic seaboard. On the Californian coast there are also a harbor porpoise, a common dolphin, and a striped porpoise, which are very abundant.

None of the large whalebone whales—the right whales, hump-backs, fin-backs, and sulphur-bottoms—can be said to be abundant on the coasts of the United States at the present day.

There are doubtless persons in many of the Atlantic fishing-towns who have had opportunities for observing the different Atlantic species under various conditions, and it is much to be regretted that more observations have not been recorded. The writings of Scammon have extended the general knowledge of the species occurring on the west coast far beyond that of those on the east coast.

There are certain names which have been used to designate so many different kinds of whales and porpoises that they ought to be avoided as much as possible. For example, the name "grampus" has been applied both to porpoises and to whales with whalebone, which are not more closely related than a horse and a cow. The word "blackfish" has been employed for any porpoise which is black. In reality the word "grampus" ought to be applied only to porpoises like that represented in fig. 17, pl. vi, and "blackfish" only to porpoises like that represented in fig. 18, pl. vi.

GENERAL OBSERVATIONS.

OBSERVATIONS ON LIVING SPECIMENS.—There are many general observations of value which may be made by voyagers and other observers, even when the species under observation cannot be exactly identified. Such relate, for example, to—

1. The number of individuals in a school.
2. The apparent equality or inequality of age and size of individuals of a school.
3. The movements in swimming, whether rolling, leaping, or otherwise.
4. The direction of the movement and the succession of different schools.

5. The rate of movement.

6. The rate of spouting or " blowing " and the phenomena accompanying that action, such as whistling, &c., or the height to which the column of spray is thrown.

Observations in the direction in which schools of the various species move at different seasons of the year are especially desirable and could be readily made by keepers of the life-saving stations and other observers on the coast.

Any observations on the breeding habits of the different species, the times of year and localities in which the young are brought forth, the size of the young at birth, the length of time they follow the mother, &c., are exceedingly important, as our knowledge on these subjects is still very defective.

Very little also is definitely known concerning the food of many species and the manner in which it is captured. Any facts bearing on this matter are well worth recording. The entire contents of the stomach should be placed in a bottle of alcohol when opportunity permits.

In addition to the few topics for investigation which have been alluded to there are many others of equal importance which will suggest themselves to the thoughtful observer. It will yet be a long time before we can say we know all that it is necessary to know about these rovers of the sea. It is indeed a strange fact that, while the external and internal peculiarities and the life-history of numberless insects and minute and lowly animals have been thoroughly investigated, many of these great beasts have been entirely neglected.

INSTRUCTIONS FOR THE USE OF THE LIFE-SAVING AND LIGHT-HOUSE SERVICES.

Stranded whales.—If a dead whale is seen floating in on the tide observe whether it is followed by porpoises and sharks or by its young.

Color.—When it strands the color of its head, back, belly, both sides of the flippers and tail, should be immediately observed and recorded.

Securing the specimen.—If the specimen is liable to be washed out to sea by succeeding tides, fasten it by the tail (*never by the flippers or jaw, unless unavoidable.*) Of course, if the specimen is small, it can be dragged up the beach out of reach of the water or even be placed in an ice-house.

Use of sand.—If the latter course cannot be taken, cover the specimen with a thick coat of *wet* sand or seaweed.

Telegraphing.—In telegraphing to Washington it is especially desirable that the following code should be used, since thereby it will be possible for the zoölogists at the Smithsonian Institution to judge of the appearance and value of specimens and to determine whether persons ought to be sent to take casts or prepare the skeleton.

Address.—All telegrams should be addressed to PROF. S. F. BAIRD, SMITHSONIAN INSTITUTION, WASHINGTON, D. C.

TELEGRAPHIC CODE.

Observe the following characters and telegraph those which are present, *using simply the numbers* instead of the words. The outlines at the left of the page are intended to aid in fixing the characters.

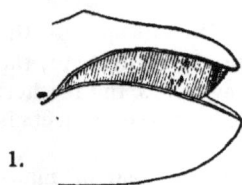

1. Whalebone in the mouth.

2. Teeth in both jaws.

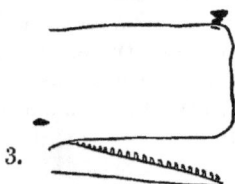

3. Teeth in the lower jaw only, but more than two or four.

4. Teeth, only two or four, at the end of the lower jaw.

5. Teeth, only two or four, in the side of the lower jaw.

6. No teeth nor whalebone in the jaws.

7. Throat smooth.

8. Throat with folds.

9. Back with a hump.

10. Back with a fin.

11. Back smooth.

12. Head rounded.

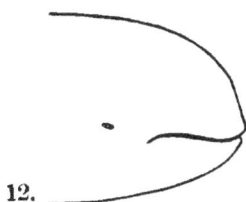

13. Head with a beak.

14. Head pointed.

Measurements.—In addition to the foregoing characters the following measurements should be recorded, and those bearing the letters A, B, E, and F (if a back-fin is present) telegraphed:

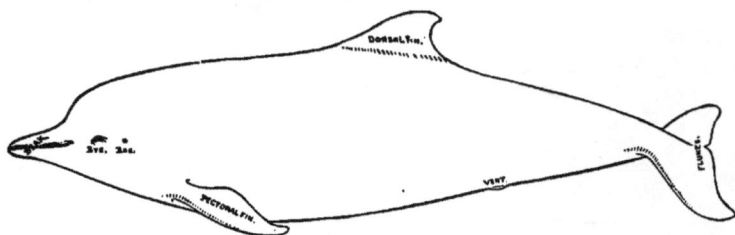

FIG. 1.—Showing the organs and regions of the body to which special names are applied.

Measurements in feet and inches.

* A. Length over all (total)...
* B. Length of the mouth.... ....
C. Breadth across the flukes from tip to tip (straight)...............
D. Depth of flukes from before backward...........................
* E. Length of flipper (pectoral fin)....................................
* F. Height of back-fin..
G. Girth at largest part ....
H. Distance from the tip of the snout to the base of the back-fin.......
I. Length of longest whalebone (when present).....................

* These are the most important measurements.

Teeth.—Also telegraph *invariably.*

Z. The total number of teeth.

The following telegram may serve as a model:

[A telegram showing the use of the symbols.]

"WESTERN UNION TELEGRAPH COMPANY,
"*Cape May, N. J., January* 1, 1885.

"Prof. S. F. BAIRD,
"*Smithsonian Institution, Washington, D. C.:*

"Female porpoise stranded near Station Ten this morning. Numbers four, seven, ten, thirteen. A, twelve feet eight inches; Z, two.

"JOHN SMITH,
"*Keeper.*"

Telegram expanded.—The foregoing telegram expanded would read as follows: "A female porpoise stranded near Life-saving Station No. 10 this morning. It has (4) teeth to the number of two or four in the lower jaw only. (7) The belly is smooth. (10) The back carries a fin. (13) The head is beaked. (A) Total length, 12 feet 8 inches. (Z) Whole number of teeth, two."

METHOD OF PACKING FRESH SPECIMENS.

Packing.—If a response is received from Washington requesting that a fresh specimen or specimens be shipped, the latter should be packed in ice, sea-weed, or sawdust.

Use of ice, sea-weed, sawdust, and salt.—Ice is almost indispensable in warm weather, but if it cannot be gotten, sea-weed may be substituted. As sea-weed is not thrown up plentifully on all parts of the coast, sawdust or even salt may be used. Sawdust should be wet.

Removing the entrails.—If specimens are packed in salt, sea-weed, or sawdust it is necessary in warm weather to remove the entrails and fill the cavity with salt. In making an opening for this purpose care should be taken not to allow the slit to extend too far toward the head, and thus to endanger the breast-bone.

SELECTIONS OF SPECIMENS FROM A SCHOOL.

In case of the stranding of a large school at a point from which it is possible to send specimens to Washington at small expense, a full-grown male and female and a young specimen should be selected. (The female may be known by the presence of a short slit on each side of the vent, in which the teats or mammæ are concealed.)

Measurements.—A few measurements of a considerable number of specimens would also be desirable.

PREPARATION OF A SKELETON.

In some cases the distance from Washington or other obstacles will prevent the sending of fresh specimens. Under such circumstances the skin and flesh should be roughly removed from the skeleton and the latter packed in dry sea-weed or sawdust. The more oily a specimen is and the longer it will be on the road the more carefully it should be cleaned. This is for the reason that the heat of the oil destroys the bones as if in a slow fire.

The hind limbs.—Special search should be made for the rudimentary bones of the hind limbs which lie in the flesh half-way between the

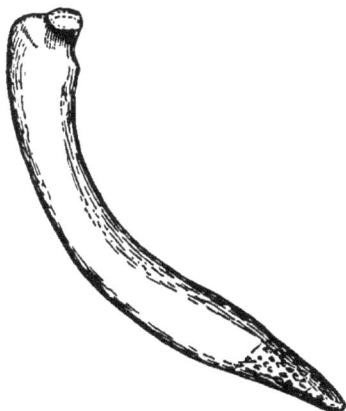

Fig. 2.—Pelvic bone of a porpoise—natural size.

backbone and the vent. The neglect to preserve these bones renders many specimens in museums imperfect. In a porpoise 6 or 8 feet long their length would not exceed 3 or 4 inches. See also page 14.

SHIPPING DIRECTIONS.

Address.—Fresh specimens should be in all cases shipped by express,* addressed to Prof. S. F. BAIRD, SMITHSONIAN INSTITUTION, WASHINGTON, D. C., and marked *"perishable."*

What to do when persons are sent from Washington.—If a response is received stating that persons will be sent to care for the specimen nothing is necessary to be done but to keep it as far as possible buried in wet sand.

INSTRUCTIONS FOR THE USE OF CAPTAINS OF WHALING-VESSELS AND OTHER OBSERVERS AND COLLECTORS.

Records.—Observers at sea having neither time nor opportunity to preserve specimens might with good result record (in a book kept for the purpose) some of the characters and measurements included in the scheme on pp. 11, 12.

Points of interest.—Among the points of interest not referred to on these pages are (*a*) the shape, color of the body, head, fins, and flukes, and the color of inside of the mouth; (*b*) the size and shape of the teeth, or the length, breadth, fineness, and color of the whalebone; (*c*) the size and color of the eye; (*d*) the size and shape of the blow-hole or blow-holes. Such observations should always be accompanied by a record of the sex of the specimen and the date upon which and the locality in which observed.

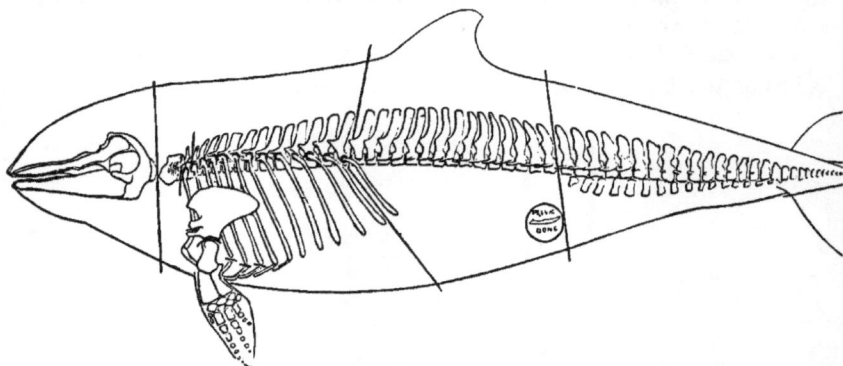

FIG. 3.—Ideal figure of a porpoise showing by cross-lines at what points the bones of the skeleton may be most conveniently separated.

The skeleton.—If specimens can be preserved, the entire skeleton is, of course, the most to be desired, provided that a record is kept of the external appearance of the animals. It is taken for granted that skeletons of very large whales cannot be preserved except under extraor-

* If too large to be boxed they should be sewed up in canvas, and thus protected on the journey.

dinary circumstances; and what follows relates to the dolphins, porpoises, and other small cetaceans.

The pelvic bones.—Care should be taken (as already intimated on a prior page) to obtain the pelvic bones or rudiments of the hind limbs which lie in the flesh on each side of and near to the vent.

The pectorals.—The flippers may be separated from the shoulder-blade by cutting close to the body and laying bare the joint; they do not need any preparation.

The flukes.—Each of the flukes should be cut off near the body (see figure 3) and thrown away.

The hind part of the body.—The tail, from the vent backwards, may be cut loose from the body in one piece, and does not need any further preparation, except in very large specimens.

The head.—The head should be severed from the body, care being taken not to injure the tongue or hyoid bones of the throat.

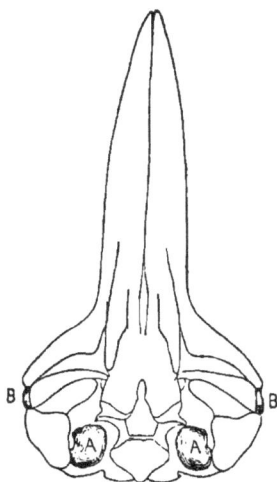

FIG. 4.—View of the under side of the skull of a whale, showing the position of A A, the ear-bones; B B, the cheek-bones.

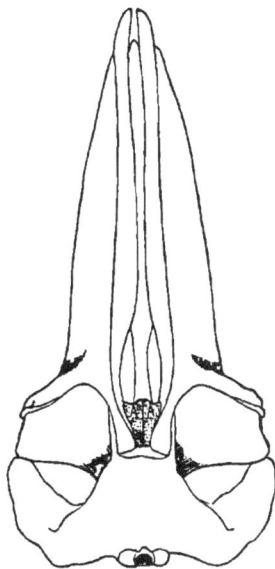

FIG. 5.—View of the upper side of the skull of a whale, showing the position of A A, the nose-bones.

The ribs.—The flesh should then be roughly removed from the head and trunk, the ribs cut loose at their junction with the backbone and with the cartilages of the breast bone.

Packing the skeleton.—The whole specimen should then be dried for a short time and packed in barrels or other receptacles with a mixture of dry saw-dust and salt, and a card or other label bearing the sex, date, and locality.

Tools.—All the operations referred to should be performed with a knife; *never with a saw or ax.*   If there is time and inclination, instead of packing the roughed-out skeleton it would be better to soak the bones in water and scrape them from time to time with a dull knife.   As already stated on p. 13, the care with which a specimen should be prepared depends upon the time which will elapse before it will reach its destination and the amount of oil which it contains.

Most desirable parts.—If it is not feasible to preserve the whole skeleton, the most desirable parts are the skull, flippers, lower jaw, ear-bones, or (in the whalebone whales) the nose-bones or pieces of whalebone.

The skull.—The skull should have the flesh roughly removed and if possible be soaked and scraped.   Care should be taken not to break the delicate malar or cheek bone which forms the lower border of the eye-socket.   The flippers need no preparation unless large; they may be dried.

Ear-bones.—The ear-bones are represented by two rounded or oblong bony masses at the back and under part of the skull.   With a little care they are readily detached.   (See fig. 4, p. 15.)

Nose-bones.—The nose-bones of the large whalebone whales lie at the extreme upper end of the great front opening of the nose, in the middle line of the skull.   In large specimens they do not exceed four or five inches in length.   They are very important in identifying species. (See fig. 5, p. 15.)

A KEY FOR THE IDENTIFICATION OF SPECIMENS.

In the subjoined key for the identification of the different tribes or genera of whales and porpoises an attempt has been made to employ only such characters as relate to the external appearance.   This is somewhat difficult for the reason that some genera which are very much alike externally differ very much internally.   Of course, the genera whose names stand near each other in this key are not necessarily closely related; in the classification which is given on page 19 an attempt is made to bring the related forms together as well as may be, when the names are placed in a line, one after another.   The figures (see plates I–XI) to which the numbers in parentheses relate are intended to show as nearly as may be the general form of some characteristic species of each genus.   They have been selected from the best figures which are to be found in the available scientific literature, and from photographs and sketches, but some are known to be imperfect. Of the genera *Agaphelus*, *Neobalæna*, and *Feresia* no figures exist.   The lengths given are those of average adult specimens.

Key to the names of genera.

[To use this key begin at *a¹*, and if the specimen in hand *agrees* with the description there given, pass to the letter with the *next figure* which stands *immediately underneath*.   If the specimen does *not* agree with the description pass instead to the *next letter of the alphabet* which bears the *same* number.]

a^1. Whalebone in the upper jaw; no teeth; blow-holes, two.

   a^2. No fin or hump on the back; no furrows on the belly.

      a^3. Whalebone very long (7 to 12 feet); color of body black.

            Balæna. Bowhead and Right whales. (32.) (Arctic and temperate seas.)

      b^3. Whalebone short (14 to 16 inches), yellow; color of body gray, mottled.

            Rhachianectes. The Gray whale. (27.) (North Pacific Ocean.)

      c^3. Whalebone short and white; color of body black above; base of pectorals white, tips black..*Agaphelus.* Scragg whale. (North Atlantic Ocean.)

            Neobalæna. Pygmy bowhead. [Only the bones and whalebone known.] (New Zealand.)

   b^2. A hump on the back; furrows on the belly; pectorals as long as the head.

            Megaptera. Humpback whales. (28.) (All seas.)

   c^2. A fin on the back. Furrows on the belly. Pectorals shorter than the head.

      d^3. Fin on the back about as near to the head as to the tail. A band of white across the pectoral (?).

            Balænoptera. Piked whales. (29.) (All seas.)

      e^3. Fin on the back much nearer to the tail than to the head.

            Physalus and *Sibbaldius.* Fin-back and sulphur-bottom whales. (30 and 31.) (All seas.)

b^1. No whalebone in the mouth.

   d^2. No teeth. One (or occasionally two) twisted tusk 5 to 8 feet long, protruding from the jaw. Color of the body light, mottled.

            Monodon. The Narwhal. (15.) (Arctic Seas.)

   e^2. No long tusk. No visible teeth in either jaw. Head with a beak. A small fin on the back nearer to the tail than to the head. Size rather large (16 to 33 feet).

            Hyperoödon (26). *Ziphius* (female and young male); *Mesoplodon* (female and young male). (24.) Bottle-nosed whales. (All seas.)

   f^2. Teeth in the lower jaw only.

      f^3. Visible teeth only *two*; in the *tip* of the lower jaw.

            Ziphius (adult male). Bottled-nosed whales. (23.) (All seas.)

      g^3. Visible teeth only *two*; in the *side* of the lower jaw.

            Mesoplodon (adult male). Bottle-nosed whales. (24a.) (North Atlantic and North Pacific Oceans.)

      h^3. Visible teeth only *four*; near the tip of the lower jaw.

            Berardius. (adult male). (25.) (New Zealand and Bering Island.)

      i^3. Teeth 6 to 14, not sharp-pointed. Head rounded. Fin at the middle of the back; moderate.

            Grampus. The grampuses. (17.) (Temperate seas.)

      j^3. Teeth 18 to 30, very sharp-pointed. Head pointed. Fin on the back nearer to the tail than to the head; small.

            Kogia. Pygmy sperm whale. (22.) (Temperate and tropical seas.)

k^3. Teeth 40 to 50; very large and blunt. Head square. Blow-holes at the end of the snout. Body very large.

Physeter. The sperm whale. (21.) (Temperate and tropical seas.)

g^2. Teeth in both jaws.

l^3. Head without a distinct long beak and more or less rounded and globular.

a^4. Teeth flattened.

a^5. A fin on the back.

Phocæna. Common porpoises; puffing pigs. (12.) (Coasts of all continents.)

b^5. No fin on the back.

Neomeris. Finless porpoises. (13.) (Indian Ocean and coast of Japan.)

b^4. Teeth round.

c^5. A fin on the back.

a^6. Teeth from 16 to 24 in each jaw.

a^7. Fin on the back much higher than the pectorals are long.

Orca. Killers. (20.) (All seas.)

b^7. Fin on the back moderate.

a^8. Head very round. Row of teeth not extending to the corner of the mouth. Pectorals long and narrow.

Globiocephalus. Blackfish. (18.) (All seas.)

b^9. Head very round. Row of teeth extending back to the corner of the mouth. Pectorals short.

Orcella. (16.) (Coast and rivers of India.)

c^8. Head sloping. Row of teeth extending back to the corner of the mouth. Pectorals short.

Pseudorca.* (19.) (Coast of Europe and of New Zealand.)

b^6. Teeth in each jaw, 44 to 66.

c^7. Edges of the fin on the back curved (*i. e.*, the dorsal fin falcate).

Lagenorhynchus. Striped porpoises. (10.) (All seas.)

d^7. Edges of the fin on the back not curved (*i. e.*, the dorsal fin triangular).

Cephalorhynchus. (11.) (Temperate Atlantic and Pacific Oceans.)

d^5. No fin on the back. Color, white.

Beluga. The White whale. (14.) (Arctic Seas.)

m^3. Head with a distinct elongated beak.

c^4. A distinct fin on the back, not in the form of a low ridge.

e^5. Bone of the tip of the lower jaw extending as far back as the fifth or sixth tooth or much further (*i. e.*, symphysis of the mandible elongate).

c^6. Teeth about 50 in each jaw.

Steno. Long-beaked dolphins. (5.) (Temperate and tropical seas.)

d^6. Teeth about 66 in each jaw.

Sotalia. River dolphins. (4.) (Rivers of tropical America and southeastern Asia.)

e^6. Teeth from 100 to 120 in each jaw.

Pontoporia. The Pontoporia. (3.) (Coast of the Argentine Republic, South America.)

f^5. Bone of the tip of the lower jaw not extending back to the 5th or 6th tooth (*i. e.*, symphysis of the mandible not elongate).

---

* Another genus, named *Feresia*, is known only from two skulls, one of which came from the "South Seas." There are about 24 teeth in each jaw. The form will probably prove to be somewhat like that of *Pseudorca*.

f^5. Teeth about 44 in each jaw.

> *Tursiops*. Bottle-nosed dolphins. (6.) (All seas.)

g^6. Teeth from 80 to 120 in each jaw.

> *Prodelphinus* and *Delphinus*. Common dolphins. (8 and 7.) (Coasts of all continents.)

d^4. No fin on the back, or simply a low ridge.

g^5. Pectorals pointed at the end.

h^6. Teeth 50 to 70 in each jaw. A ridge on the back. Beak long.

> *Inia*. The Inia. (2.) (Upper Amazon River and tributaries, South America.)

i^6. Teeth about 80 in each jaw. Beak short.

> *Leucorhamphus*. Right-whale porpoises. (9.) (Atlantic and Pacific Oceans.)

h^5. Pectorals broad and truncated. Eyes very small ($\frac{1}{8}$ inch). Beak turned up at the end.

> *Platanista*. The Susu. (1.) (Rivers of India.)

A SYSTEMATIC ARRANGEMENT OF THE GENERA AND HIGHER DIVISIONS OF CETACEANS.

Order CETE.—Whales or Cetaceans.

Sub-order DENTICETE.—Toothed Whales.

Family PLATANISTIDÆ.—The River Dolphins.

1. *Platanista*, Wagler.—The Susu.
   The Ganges and Indus Rivers, India.
2. *Inia*, D'Orbigny.—The Inia.
   The Amazon River and its tributaries.
3. *Pontoporia*, Gray.—The Pontoporia.
   Coast of the Argentine Republic.

Family DELPHINIDÆ.—Porpoises and Dolphins.

4. *Sotalia*, Gray.—River dolphins.
   Rivers of South America and India.
5. *Steno*, Gray.—Long-beaked dolphins.
   Temperate and tropical seas.
6. *Tursiops*, Gervais.—Bottle-nosed dolphins.
   All seas.
7. *Delphinus*, Linné.—Common dolphins.
   Coasts of all continents.
8. *Prodelphinus*, Gervais.—Common dolphins.
   All seas.
9. *Leucorhamphus*, Lilljeborg.—Right-whale porpoises.
   Atlantic and Pacific Oceans.
10. *Lagenorhynchus*, Gray.—Striped dolphins.
    All seas.

11. *Cephalorhynchus*, Cuvier.—White-marked porpoises.
    Temperate Atlantic and Pacific Oceans.
12. *Phocœna*, Cuvier.—Common porpoises.
    All seas.
13. *Neomeris*, Gray.
    Indian Ocean and coast of Japan.
14. *Delphinapterus*, Lacépède.—The Beluga or White whale.
    Arctic seas.
15. *Monodon*, Linné.—The Narwhal.
    Arctic seas.
16. *Orcella*, Gray.
    Rivers and coast of India.
17. *Grampus*, Gray.—Grampuses.
    Temperate seas.
18. *Globiocephalus*, Lesson.—Blackfish.
    All seas.
19. *Pseudorca*, Reinhardt.—False killers.
    Northern Europe; Tasmania.
20. *Orca*, Gray.—Killers.
    All seas.
20a. *Feresia*, Gray.

Family PHYSETERIDÆ.—The Sperm whales.

21. *Physeter*, Linné.—The Sperm whale.
    Temperate and tropical seas.
22. *Kogia*, Gray.—The Pygmy Sperm whale.
    Temperate and tropical seas.

Family ZIPHIIDÆ.—Bottle-nose whales.

23. *Ziphius*, Cuvier.
    All seas.
24. *Mesoplodon*, Gervais.
    Atlantic and Pacific Oceans.
25. *Berardius*, Duvernoy.—Berard's whale.
    New Zealand; Bering Island.
26. *Hyperoödon*, Lacépède.—Bottle-nose whale.
    North Atlantic Ocean.

Suborder MYSTICETE.—The Whalebone whales.

Family BALÆNIDÆ.

27. *Rhachianectes*, Cope.—The Devil-fish or Gray whale.
    North Pacific Ocean.
27a. *Agaphelus*, Cope.—The Scragg whale (?)
    North Atlantic Ocean.

28. *Megaptera*, Gray.—Humpback whales.
     All seas.
29. *Balænoptera*, Lacépède.—Piked whales.
     All seas.
30. *Physalus*, Gray.—Fin-back whales.
     All seas.
31. *Sibbaldius*, Gray.—Sulphur-bottom whales.
     All seas.
32. *Balæna*, Linné.—Bowhead and Right whales.
     Arctic and temperate seas.
33. *Neobalæna*, Gray.—Pygmy Bowhead.
     New Zealand seas.

A CHECK-LIST OF THE SPECIES OF CETACEANS WHICH
OCCUR ON THE COASTS OF NORTH AMERICA.

Order CETE.

Suborder DENTICETE.

Family DELPHINIDÆ.

Sotalia pallida, Gervais. Florida (?)
? *Steno fuscus*, Gray. Cuba.
Steno compressus, Gray. Gulf of Mexico (?)
Delphinus Bairdii, Dall. Baird's Dolphin. Coast of California.
Delphinus delphis, Linné. Common Dolphin. Atlantic Ocean.
? *Delphinus albirostratrus*, Peale.
Delphinus janira, Gray. The Janira. Newfoundland. (Gray.)
? *Prodelphinus euphrosyne*, (Gray) True. North Atlantic Ocean.
? *Leucorhamphus borealis*, (Peale) Gill. Right-whale Porpoise. Pacific
     coast of North America.
Lagenorhynchus acutus, Gray. Eschricht's Dolphin. North Atlantic
     Ocean.
Lagenorhynchus albirostris, Gray. White-beaked Bottlenose. North
     Atlantic Ocean.
Lagenorhynchus obliquidens, Gill. Striped or common Dolphin. Pacific coast of the United States.
? *Lagenorhynchus tricolea*, Gray. West coast of North America.
Lagenorhynchus gubernator, Cope. Skunk Porpoise. Coast of New
     England.
Lagenorhynchus perspicillatus, Cope. Coast of New England.
Tursiops tursio, (Bonnaterre) Van Ben. and Gervais. Bottle-nose Dolphin. North Atlantic Ocean.
Tursiops Gillii, Dall. Cow-fish. Pacific coast of the United States.

Tursiops erebennus, (Cope) Gill. Black Dolphin. Atlantic coast of the United States.

Orca gladiator, (Bonnaterre) Gray. Atlantic Killer. Atlantic Ocean.

Orca atra, Cope. Pacific Killer. Pacific coast of North America.

? *Orca pacifica,* Gray. North Pacific Ocean.

Globiocephalus melas, (Traill). Blackfish. North Atlantic Ocean.

Globiocephalus brachypterus, Cope. Coast of New Jersey.

Globiocephalus Scammoni, Cope. Pacific coast of North America and southwards.

Grampus griseus, (Cuvier) Gray. Grampus. North Atlantic Ocean.

Grampus Stearnsii, Dall. Mottled or White-headed Grampus. Pacific coast of North America.

Delphinapterus catodon, (Linné) Gill. White Whale. Arctic and Sub-arctic seas.

Monodon monoceros, Linné. Narwhal. Arctic seas.

Phocœna communis, Lesson. Puffing Pig. Herring Hog. North Atlantic Ocean.

Phocœna lineata, Cope. Striped Porpoise. Atlantic coast of the United States.

Phocœna vomerina, Gill. California Bay Porpoise. Pacific coast of the United States.

Family ZIPHIIDÆ.—Bottle-nosed Whales.

Berardius Grebnitzkii, Stejneger. Bering Island.

Hyperoodon rostratum, (Chemnitz) Wesmael. Bottle-nose Whale. North Atlantic Ocean.

Ziphius cavirostris, Cuvier. Temperate and tropical seas.

? *Ziphius semijunctus,* (Cope). Atlantic Ocean.

Ziphius Bairdii, Stejneger. Baird's Bottle-nose Whale. Bering Island.

Mesoplodon Sowerbiensis, Gervais. Temperate north Atlantic.

Family PHYSETERIDÆ.—The Sperm Whales.

Physeter macrocephalus, Linné. Sperm Whale. Temperate and tropical seas.

Kogia breviceps, (De Blainville) Gray. Pygmy Sperm Whale. Temperate and tropical seas.

Suborder MYSTICETE.—The Whalebone Whales.

Family BALÆNIDÆ.

Rhachianectes glaucus, Cope. Devil-fish; Gray Whale. Pacific coast of North America.

Agaphelus gibbosus, Cope. Scragg Whale. North Atlantic.

Megaptera longimana (Rudolphi), Gray. Humpback Whale. North Atlantic Ocean.

Megaptera bellicosa, Cope. Caribbean Sea.

Megaptera versabilis, Cope. Humpback Whale. Pacific coast of North
   America.

Physalus antiquorum, Gray. Finback Whale; Razor-back. North Atlantic Ocean.

Balænoptera rostratus, (Müller) Gray. Pike Whale (? Grampus of New
   England fishermen). North Atlantic Ocean.

Balænoptera Davidsoni, Scammon. Finback Whale. Northwestern
   coast of the United States.

? *Balænoptera robustus*, Lilljeborg. Gräsö Whale. North Atlantic
   Ocean.

Sibbaldius laticeps, Gray. Rudolphi's Rorqual. North Atlantic Ocean.

Sibbaldius sulfureus, Cope. Sulphur bottom Whale. Pacific coast of
   North America.

Sibbaldius velifera, (Cope). Finback Whale. Pacific coast of North
   America.

Sibbaldius tuberosus, Cope. Mobjack Bay, Virginia.

Sibbaldius tectirostris, Cope. Coast of Maryland.

Balæna japonica, Gray. Right Whale of the North Pacific. North
   Pacific Ocean.

Balæna biscayensis, Gray. Black Whale. Right Whale of the North
   Atlantic. Temperate North Atlantic.

Balæna mysticetus, Linné. Bowhead Whale. Arctic seas.

PLATE I.

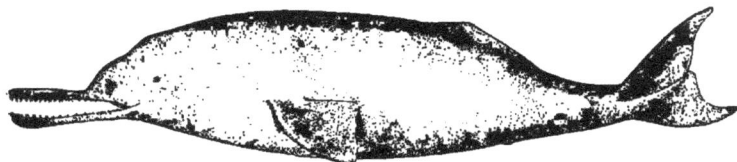

1. *Platanista gangetica*, (Lebeck) Wagler.   The Susu.
Length, 8 feet.   (After Eschricht.)

2. *Inia Geoffroyi*, (Desmarest) Gray.   The Inia.   (Young specimen.)
Length, 8 feet.   (After F. Cuvier.)

3. *Pontoporia Blainvillei*, (Gervais) Gray.   The Pontoporia.
Length, 5 feet.   (After Malm.)

GENERA OF CETACEANS.

PLATE II.

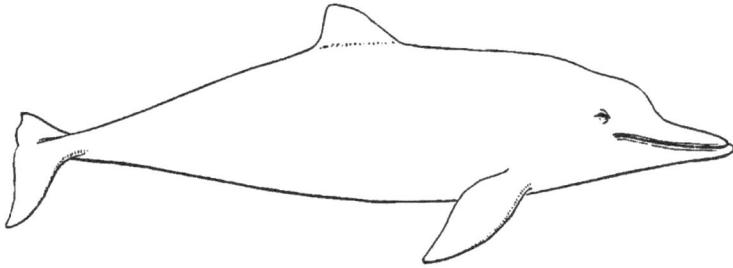

4. *Sotalia fluviatilis,* (Gervais). River Dolphin.
Length, 5 feet. (After Gervais.)

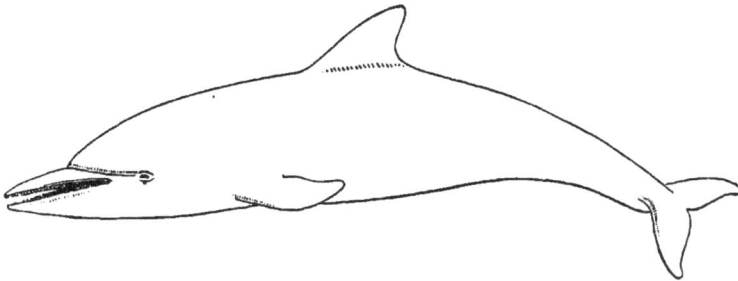

5. *Steno perspicillatus,* Peters. Long-beaked Dolphin.
Length, 8 feet. (?) (After Peters.)

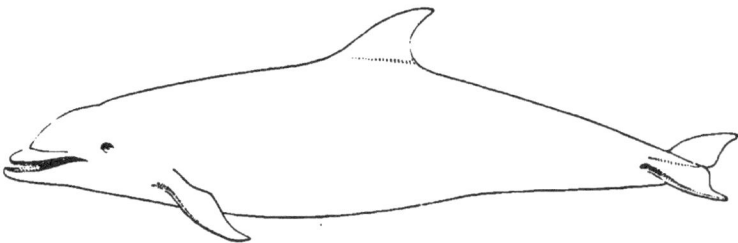

6. *Tursiops tursio,* (Bonnaterre) Van Ben. and Gervais. Common Bottle-
nose Dolphin.
Length, 11 feet. (After Flower.)

GENERA OF CETACEANS.

7. *Delphinus delphis*, Linné.   Common Dolphin.
Length, 6½ feet.   (From a sketch by J. H. Emerton.)

8. *Prodelphinus punctatus*, (Gray) True.   Spotted Dolphin.
Length, 6 feet.   (After Gray.)

9. *Leucorhamphus borealis*, (Peale) Dall.   Right-whale Porpoise.
Length, 8 feet.   (From a sketch by William H. Dall.)

GENERA OF CETACEANS.

PLATE V.

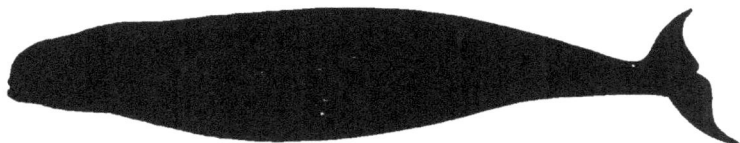

13. *Neom ris phocœnoïdes*, (Cuvier) Gray. The Nameno-juo.
Length, 4 feet. (After Schlegel.)

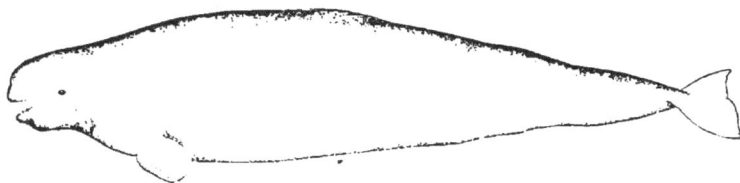

14. *Delphinopterus leucas*, (Pallas). White Whale.
Length, 12 feet. (After a photograph by the U. S. Fish Commission.)

15. *Monodon monoceros*, Linné. Narwhal.
Length of body, 16 feet; length of tusk, 8 feet. (Modified from F. Cuvier.)

GENERA OF CETACEANS.

PLATE VI.

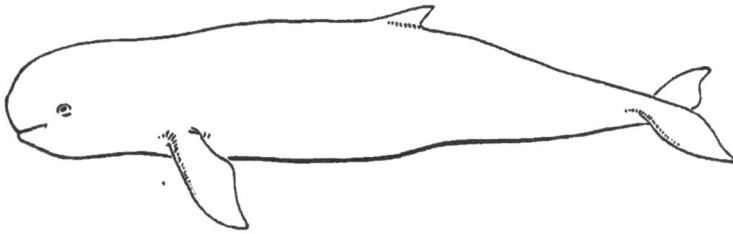

16. *Orcella fluminalis*, Anderson.   Indian River-dolphin.
Length, 6 feet. (?)   (After Anderson.)

17. *Grampus grisens*, (Cuvier) Gray.   Grampus.
Length, 10 feet 6 inches.   (After Flower.)

18. *Globiocephalus melas*, (Traill).   Blackfish.
Length, 19 feet.   (After Flower.)

GENERA OF CETACEANS.

PLATE VII.

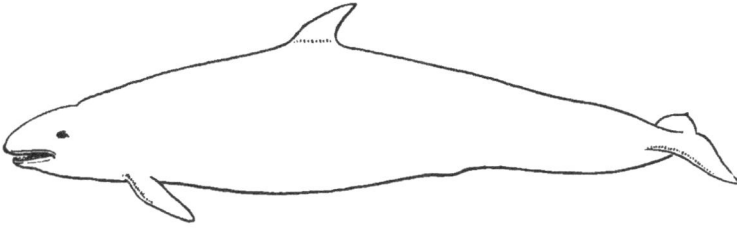

' 19. *Pseudorca crassidens*, (Owen) Reinhardt. False Killer.
Length, 16 feet. (After Reinhardt.)

20. *Orca atra*, Cope. Killer.
Length, 20 feet. (After Scammon.)

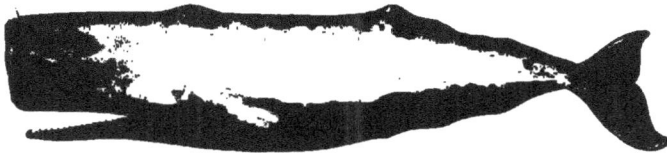

21. *Physeter catodon*, Linné. Sperm Whale.
Length, 60 feet. (After Scammon.)

GENERA OF CETACEANS.

22. *Kogia breviceps*, (Blainville) Gray.   Pygmy Sperm Whale.

Length, 8 feet, 6 inches.   (From photographs by the U. S. Fish Commission of a specimen captured at the U. S. Life Saving Station, Spring Lake, New Jersey, and now in the U. S. National Museum.)

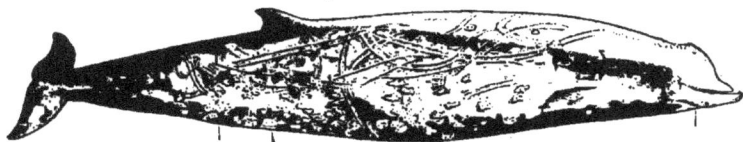

23. *Ziphius novæ-zealandiæ*, Von Haast.
Length, 20 feet.   (After Von Haast.)

24. *Mesoplodon Sowerbiensis*, (Blainville) Gervais.   Sowerby's Whale, female.
Length, 11 feet.   (After Dumortier.)

24a. Head of male Sowerby's Whale.
(After Andrews.)

GENERA OF CETACEANS.

25. *D. rardius Arnuxi*, Duvernoy.   Arnux's Whale.
Length, 20 feet.   (After Knox.)

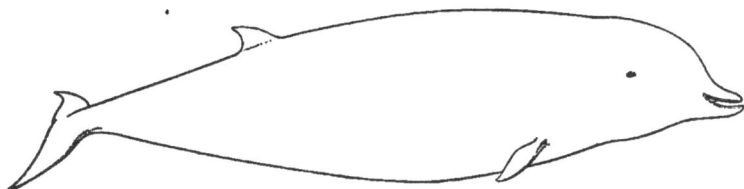

26. *Hyperoodon rostratus*, (Chemnitz) Wesmael.   Bottlenose Whale.   (Female.)
Length, 30 feet.   (After Wesmael.)

27. *Rhachianectes glaucus*, Cope.   California Gray Whale.
Length, 44 feet.   (After Scammon.)

GENERA OF CETACEANS.

28. *Megaptera versabilis*, Cope.   Pacific Humpback Whale.
Length, 48 feet.   (After Scammon.)

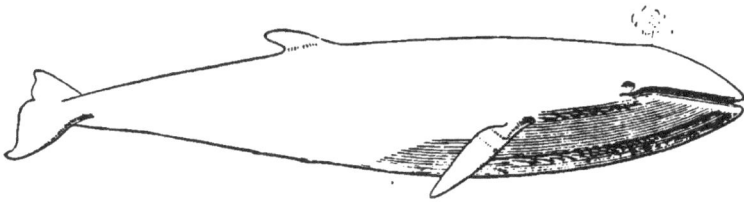

29. *Balænoptera Davidsoni*, Cope.   Little Piked Whale.
Length, 30 feet.   (After Scammon.)

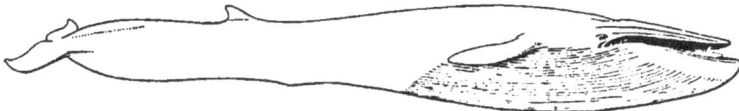

30. *Physalus antiquorum*, Gray.   Common Fin-back Whale.
Length, 70 feet.   (After Sars.)

GENERA OF CETACEANS.

Report U. S. F. C. 1883.—True. Cetaceans.

PLATE XL

31. *Sibbaldius reliferus*, (Cope). Pacific Finback Whale.
Length, 80 feet. (After Scammon.)

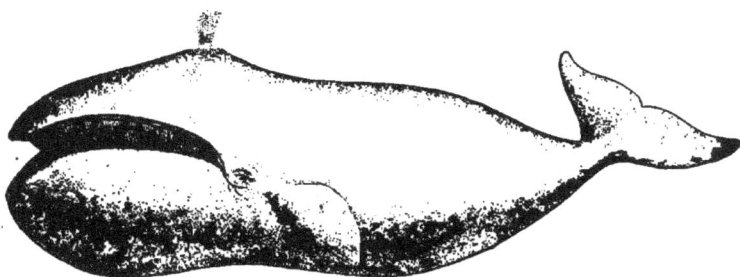

32. *Balæna mysticetus*, Linné. Bowhead Whale.
Length, 60 feet. (After Scammon.)

GENERA OF CETACEANS.

INDEX.

[25]